LIFE ON ANCIENT EARTH

AGE OF THE DINOSAURS

Christian Lopetz

Cherry Lake Press

Published in the United States of America by Cherry Lake Publishing Group
Ann Arbor, Michigan

www.cherrylakepublishing.com

Reading Adviser: Beth Walker Gambro, MS, Ed., Reading Consultant, Yorkville, IL

Photo Credits:
© Warpaint/Shutterstock (T rex), © Daniel Eskridge/Shutterstock (Triceratops), cover; colored border at bottom and top © Mj_arch/Shutterstock, cover and throughout book; © Art Posting/Shutterstock (background pattern art), back cover and throughout book; ; © mentalmind/Shutterstock, (rock sidebar art throughout book); P4/5: © Orla/Shutterstock, © Warpaint/Shutterstock, © ChocoPie/Shutterstock; P6/7: © Rattana/Shutterstock, © Noiel/Shutterstock, © Dotted Yeti/Shutterstock, © Orla/Shutterstock; P8/9: © Elenarts/Shutterstock, © Dotted Yeti/Shutterstock, © Oleg and Polly/Shutterstock, © Rainer Lesniewski/Shutterstock (Pangea); P10-11 Eoraptor © Stocktrek Images/Shutterstock, Mussaurus © YuRi Photolife/Shutterstock, Coloradisaurus © Adwo/Shutterstock, © Lubo Ivanko/Shutterstock (background); P12/13 © 3dMediSphere/Shutterstock, © Liu zishan/Shutterstock; P14/15 © Herschel Hoffmeyer/Shutterstock, © Herschel Hoffmeyer/Shutterstock, © Dotted Yeti/Shutterstock; P16/17 © Daniel Eskridge/Shutterstock, © mitsuap/Shutterstock, © Herschel Hoffmeyer/Shutterstock, © Orla/Shutterstock; P18/19 © Dotted Yeti/Shutterstock, © Innakote/Shutterstock, Shutterstock AI; P20/21 © 3dMediSphere/Shutterstock, © Marques/Shutterstock, © Warpaint/Shutterstock, © Ungar-Biewer/Shutterstock; P22/23 © Mariana_Rusanovschi/Shutterstock, © Ton Ponchai/Shutterstock, © CLOUD-WALKER/Shutterstock (Geologic Time Chart).

Produced for Cherry Lake Publishing by bluedooreducation.com

Cherry Lake Press is an imprint of Cherry Lake Publishing Group.

Library of Congress Cataloging-in-Publication Data has been filed and is available at catalog.loc.gov.

Printed in the United States of America

Note from Publisher: Websites change regularly, and their future contents are outside of our control. Supervise children when conducting any recommended online searches for extended learning opportunities.

ABOUT THE AUTHOR

From animal habitats to the solar system, Christian has written several science books for young kids. When he's not busy writing books—or music—he's a part-time dinosaur fanatic studying up on the latest dinosaur news, and watching Jurassic Park for the 65 millionth time! He lives and works in Los Angeles as a music composer.

CONTENTS

WELCOME, TIME TRAVELERS!

Let's travel back millions of years to meet some of the wildest, most wonderful creatures to ever walk the Earth—DINOSAURS!

Stegosaurus

We will find the answers to some big questions, such as:

- Why did dinosaurs go **extinct**?
- Which dino had the biggest bite?
- Who are the dinosaur relatives still living today?

Tyrannosaurus rex, also called *T. rex*

DIG THIS!

Before 1842, the word *dinosaur* did not exist. People had found dinosaur **fossils**, but thought they were from dragons or other mythical creatures. In 1842, Sir Richard Owen, an English biologist, classified them as dinosauria, which means *terrible lizard*.

Parasaurolophus

Grab your adventure gear! We are going to travel through three important time periods: Triassic, Jurassic, and Cretaceous. They are parts of the Mesozoic Era.

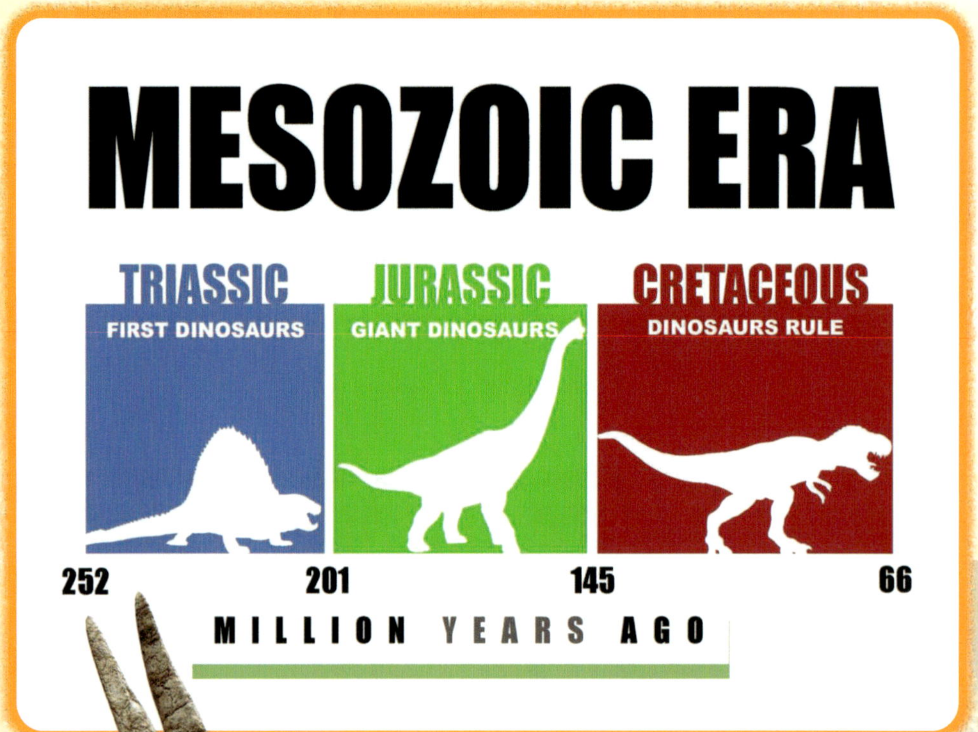

Triceraptops lived during the late Cretaceous period.

DAWN OF THE DINOSAURS

DINO TIME LOG

TRIASSIC PERIOD

252–201 million years ago

The very beginning of the age of dinosaurs

The Triassic Period is the first of three dinosaur time periods.

Each time we land in a new dinosaur age, check the Dino Time Logs for important information!

A herd of *Plateosauruses*

The Triassic Period was hot and rocky. Only a few plants grew. Most of Earth's land back then was all connected as one giant continent. It was a harsh place to live.

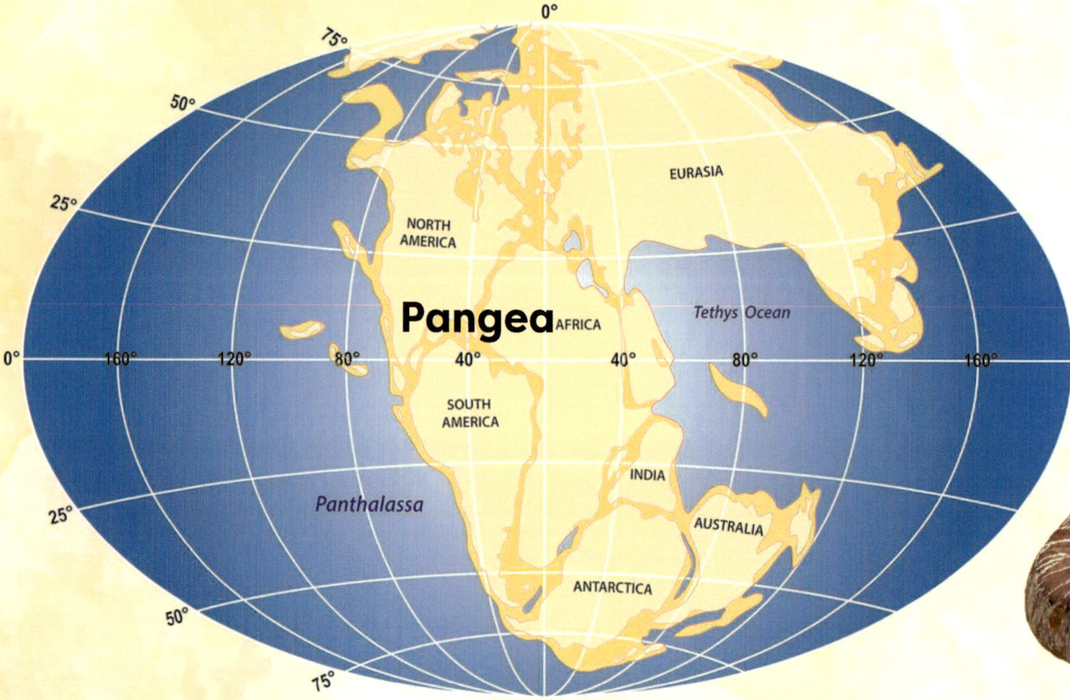

DIG THIS!

In 1912, Alfred Wegener, a German scientist, named the Earth's ancient giant continent *Pangea*. He believed that over millions of years, Pangea broke and drifted apart into the continents we know today.

Triassic dinosaurs were small. They didn't weigh much. But they were quick. Four of these early dinosaurs were *Plateosaurus, Eoraptor, Mussaurus,* and *Coloradisaurus.*

DINO Highlight

PLATEOSAURUS

Plateosaurus was one of the first dinosaurs scientists named. At 15–30 feet (4.5–9 meters) long, it was no small fry. Don't worry, it was an **herbivore**, meaning it only ate plants.

Name: *Plateosaurus*
Pronunciation: pla-tee-uh-SAW-ruhs
Lived: 214-204 million years ago
Length: 15-30 feet (5-10 m)

Eoraptor means “dawn thief” because it was one of the earliest dinosaurs to ever live. It probably hunted insects and little animals.

Mussaurus means “mouse lizard,” but don’t let the name fool you. Grown-ups could grow over 20 ft (6 m) long! Scientists first found only baby fossils of *Mussaurus*, which is how it got its tiny sounding name.

Coloradisaurus was another Triassic dinosaur. It was small and ate plants. It walked on two legs. It got its name because it was found in the Los Colorados Formation, a rock formation in Argentina, not Colorado.

Eorapter

A life-sized model of a *Coloradisaurus* with a life-sized model of a *Zupaysaurus* in the foreground

These may have been the first dinosaurs to walk the Earth, but get ready. Things are about to get bigger, louder, and leafier.

Next stop, the Jurassic Period!

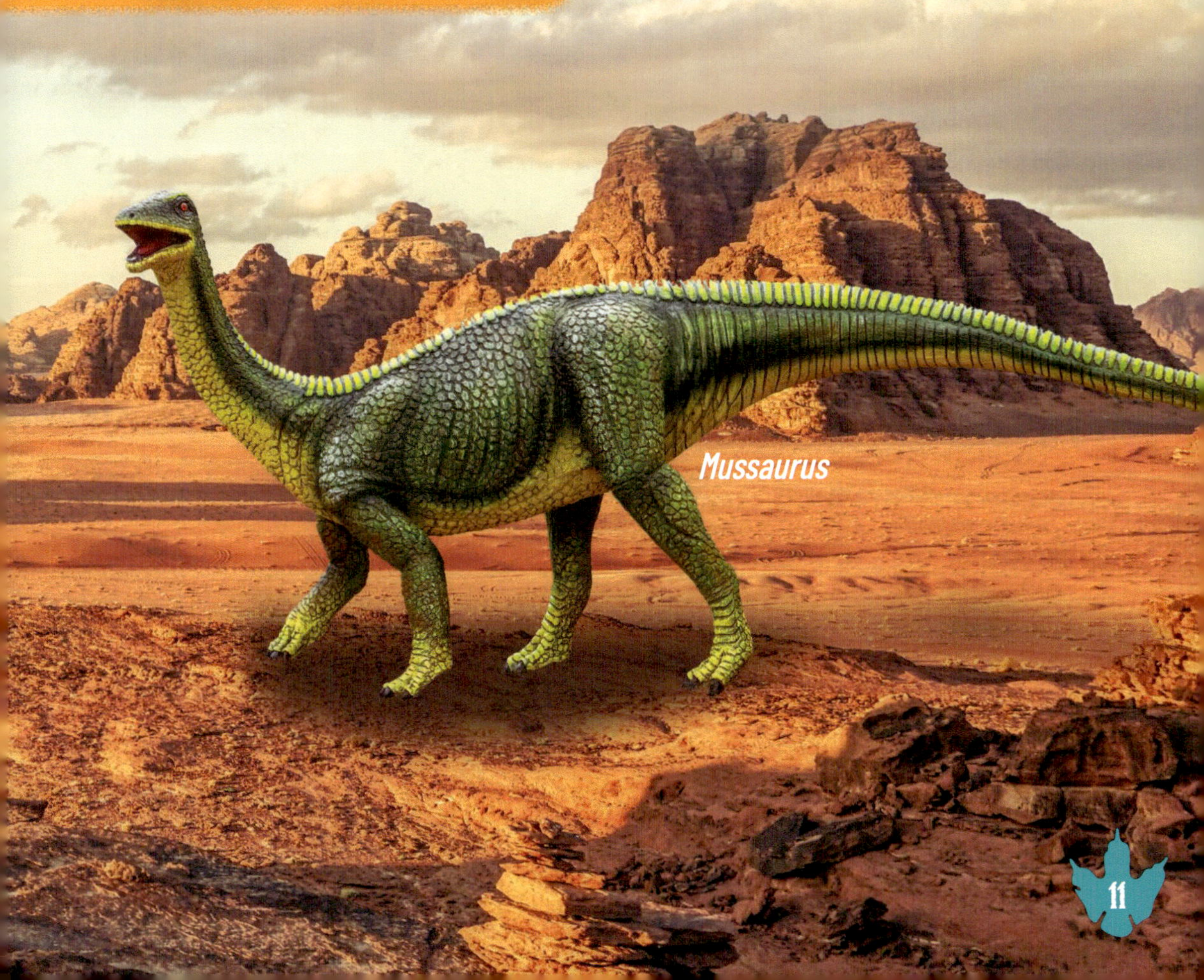

RISE OF THE DINOSAURS

DINO TIME LOG

JURASSIC PERIOD
201–145 million years ago
The second age of the dinosaurs

The Jurassic Period was warmer and wetter than the Triassic Period. Plants sprouted. Huge forests grew up. These jungles had plenty of food for plant-eating dinosaurs. The meat-eating dinosaurs that ate the herbivores also thrived.

DINO Highlight

STEGOSAURUS

Stegosaurus was a large herbivore with big plates on its back. It also had a spiked tail for protection from **predators**.

Diplodocus, a plant eater, had a long neck and a long, whip-like tail.

Name: *Stegosaurus*
Pronunciation: steg-uh-SAW-ruhs
Lived: 155-150 million years ago
Length: 20-30 feet (6-10 m)

DIG THIS!

Dinos didn't rule alone in the Jurassic period. Flying reptiles soared through the skies, and early marine reptiles swam in the seas.

Allosaurus was one of the top predators of the Jurassic Period. It had sharp teeth and three claws on each hand. It was like an older cousin of *T. rex*. It wasn't as big, but still scary.

Allosaurus

Also from this period was *Brachiosaurus*. It was a gentle giant with a very long neck. This was perfect for munching leaves from tall trees. Its front legs were longer than its back legs, which also helped it reach the tallest branches for food.

Another Jurassic dinosaur was *Archaeopteryx*. It was one of the first feathered dinosaurs to be discovered. It could even fly short distances. Through fossils, we know that many dinosaurs had feathers, and *Archaeopteryx* was the first clue!

Archaeopteryx

Brachiosaurus

AGE OF THE DINOSAURS

During the Cretaceous Period, Earth looked more like it does today. Time travelers like us would recognize forests, mountains, and even snowy places.

DINO TIME LOG

CRETACEOUS PERIOD

145–66 million years ago

The last age of the dinosaurs

Ankylosaurus

DINO Highlight

SPINOSAURUS

Spinosaurus was one of the biggest **carnivores**, meaning it ate only meat. It had a huge sail on its back. This hefty hunter used its long jaws mostly to snap up fish.

Name: *Spinosaurus*
Pronunciation: spy-nuh-SAW-ruhs
Lived: 99-93 million years ago
Length: 45-60 feet (14-18 m)

Velociraptor was small, fast, and covered in feathers. It used its curved toe claw like a hook to grab prey.

Triceratops had three sharp horns and a giant frill on its head. This dino looked scary, but it ate only plants.

Flowers grew and tiny mammals lived alongside dinosaurs in Cretaceous times. More birds also began to appear.

DINO Highlight

TYRANNOSAURUS REX

T. rex is one of the most famous dinosaurs of all time. It was a powerful predator with jaws full of sharp teeth.

Even though it had tiny arms, its bite was one of the strongest of any land animal in history.

Name: *Tyrannosaurus rex*
Pronunciation: ty-ran-uh-SAW-ruhs REX
Lived: 83-66 million years ago
Length: 40 feet (12 m)

DEEP TIME: 66 MILLION YEARS AGO

A huge **asteroid** hit Earth, causing a worldwide climate shift. Many dinosaurs and other animals on land and sea died out.

A giant asteroid fell to Earth and ended the Cretaceous Period. Everything changed. It caused fires, blocked sunlight, and caused most of the dinosaurs to go extinct.

How do we know so much about dinosaurs? Fossils!

Fossils form when a plant or dead animal gets buried in mud or sand. It takes over ten thousand years for a fossil to form.

How is a fossil made? Over time, the animal or plant's soft parts rot away. Minerals take their place and form a copy in stone.

Old bones, teeth, eggs, and even poop can become fossils. Footprints and patterns from feathers or plants can become fossils, too. We call these **trace fossils.**

By studying fossils, scientists can learn what dinosaurs looked like, what they ate, and even how they moved.

Dinosaurs may be gone, but their story lives on in fossils and in curious explorers like you!

DIG THIS!

Not all dinosaurs disappeared. Some of them **evolved** into modern-day birds.

GEOLOGIC TIMELINE

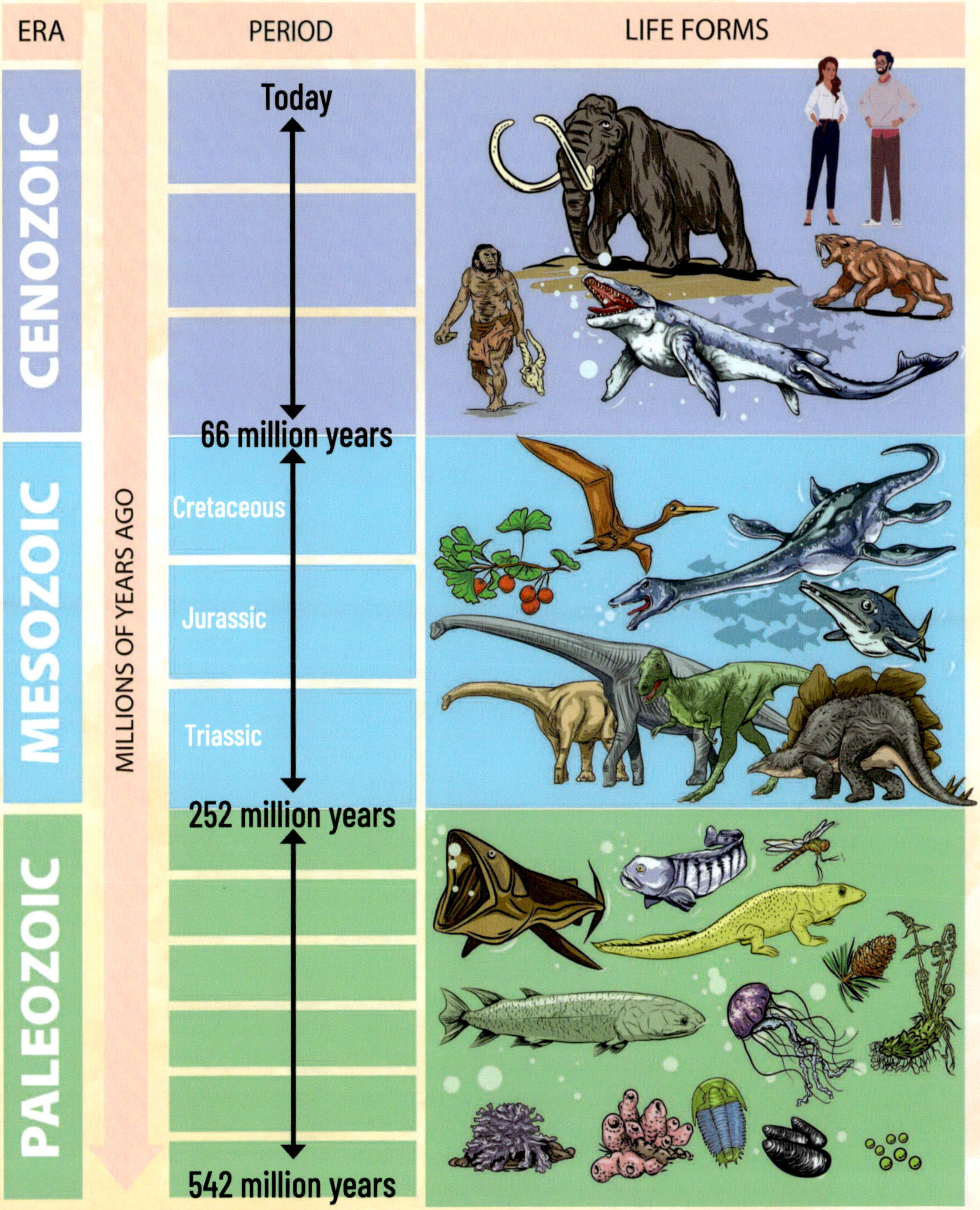

Scientists divide Earth's history into eras to help them organize Earth's past and study how life has changed. Each section marks important events, like when new life appeared or when many plants and animals went extinct.

FIND OUT MORE

BOOKS

Hulick, Kathryn. *Dinosaurs.* North Mankato, MN: Abdo Publishing, 2023.

Murray, Laura K. *Triceratops.* North Mankato, MN: Pebble, Capstone, 2025.

WEBSITES

Search these online sources with an adult:

National Geographic Kids | Tyrannosaurus rex

Natural History Museum, UK | The Rise of The Dinosaurs

GLOSSARY

asteroid (AS-tuh-royd) a giant space rock

carnivores (KAHR-nuh-vorz) animals that eat only meat

evolved (ih-VAHLVD) changed slowly and naturally over time

extinct (ik-STINGKT) no longer found alive

fossils (FAH-sulz) the hard remains or shapes of plants or animals from long ago

herbivore (UR-buh-vor) an animal that eats only plants

Pangea (pan-JEE-uh) a supercontinent made up of almost all the land on Earth before it broke apart millions of years ago

predators (PRED-uh-turz) animals that hunt and eat other animals for food

trace fossils (TRAYS FAH-sulz) the hard remains of shapes or patterns from life long ago, such as footprints or leaf patterns

INDEX